FAIRACRES PUBLICATIONS 192

# JESUS
# THE UNDISTORTED IMAGE OF GOD

JOHN TOWNROE

SLG Press
Convent of the Incarnation
Fairacres, Parker Street
Oxford OX4 1TB
www.slgpress.co.uk

First Edition 2022

Fairacres Publications No. 192

Print ISBN 978-0-7283-0322-5
Fairacres Publications Series ISSN 0307-1405



Edited and typeset in Palatino Linotype by Julia Craig-McFeely

*Acknowledgements*:
Text transcribed from talks given at a retreat 7–10 July 1992 for former students of St Boniface College, Warminster.

SLG Press
Convent of the Incarnation
Fairacres • Oxford
www.slgpress.co.uk

Printed by
Grosvenor Group Ltd, Loughton, Essex

# CONTENTS

# PREFACE

The addresses which follow were originally given to eighty former students of St Boniface College Warminster, which provided a fourth year of training for ordination to men (then) who had already completed three years of study at King's College London. The Revd Canon E. John Townroe was first chaplain (1948–1956) then warden of this College (1956–1969), and more than a thousand students came under his care during his twenty-one years there.

When this fourth year was eventually discontinued, an annual summer retreat was begun in the same premises which were now used by a school; this included the Chapel in which John Townroe had so often addressed the ordinands. After many years he was invited to lead one of these retreats and it was over-subscribed, a testament to the great affection and respect in which John was held. Of course there were resonances peculiar to those attendees: shared memories, a depth of affection and a characteristic humour evident from the original opening words, "Well, here we are again! You there, me here!"; John's humility was also evident in his description of the experience of talking to so many of his former students as "wonderful and awesome".

The material is nevertheless of wide application to lay and ordained alike and, as far as possible in book form, the text is faithful to the original. This is in the good hope, and indeed confidence, that some of the power of the words and something of John's sweetness of spirit can communicate itself to the reader now, as it undoubtedly did to those present at the time.

SR CAROL CHN

# JESUS
# THE UNDISTORTED
# IMAGE OF GOD

# 1
# INTRODUCTION

God's hand has guided us, guarded us, down the years to this day which the Lord has made. So let us rejoice and be glad in it, and let us launch out into this retreat with confidence. Confidence in God who does His mighty works in such unexpected ways—He surely has some further mighty work in hand.

Each chapter is in two parts, the first being a presentation of the theme concerning Jesus, in which I will suggest at least one passage of Scripture as an anchor around which your thoughts may turn, much as a yacht at anchor turns as it is moved by the wind and tide. The second part is an application of that theme to our daily lives of prayer and interaction with God. I suggest that between the first and second parts there should be a brief time for reflection and prayer; this can be as long or as short as you like. Finally I will offer a spiritual exercise to put into practice the points that have been mentioned. Since, as well as reading this text, you may be making quiet time for God, I have put at the back of this book some notes on using this quiet time: they are quite basic notes and I offer them simply because I know for myself that I am helped by having reminders of the basics.

This introduction serves as the opening of your retreat, so the first things to consider are why you are here and what you hope this time of reflection and prayer will be for you. Here I introduce the first of my alliterative ideas: *Aim, Approach, Attitude.* Let us launch into this retreat with confidence, confidence in God who does His mighty works in such unexpected ways.

*What is the Aim of this retreat?*

My aim is that we should come face to face anew in spirit with Jesus Christ who called and calls us; that we should do this repeatedly and deliberately throughout our retreat; that in prayer and reflection we should allow Him, our Lord and Saviour, to make upon us whatever fresh impact He will. Then, led by the Spirit, we may make whatever response to God the Lord wills.

*What is our Approach to making a retreat?*

I suggest our approach needs to be one of expectation: we should move into this time expecting that God has a word somewhere in it for each of us personally; a word, a message for our own private and personal circumstances. There is something He has to say to us just where we are in life, something to give us for whatever lies ahead in life.

Shall we be ready to receive it, to 'hear' the particular Word as it may form itself in our hearts as we go along, or possibly right at the very end? In order to be ready to receive it, I believe we need at the outset to stir up our expectant faith: do I believe God has 'a word' for me, or don't I? If I do not, why am I here?

*What is our Attitude towards making a retreat?*

It is a conventional phrase. Do we have to 'make a retreat', to create it, to make the grade by efforts of our own? I like to compare our rightful effort in retreat, or indeed in any time of prayer, with what you have to do in a sailing-boat. You have to push out and set the sails if you want to get anywhere, but then you have to wait: wait for the wind to blow, to fill the sails, to carry you forward. There is effort in the pushing out, in the hoisting and the setting, and there is effort of another kind in the waiting. But the forward movement depends entirely on the wind, which cannot be manufactured, but comes as a free gift, as 'grace'.

The useful thing about this illustration is that on closer inspection you come to realize that the impulse to set sail is also something 'given', as is the energy that enables you to make the effort, so it is all grace, though in different modes.

Let us adopt this attitude straight away in our retreat-making, seeing it all as of grace, all as given, including some well-placed effort, and much waiting upon God for His Spirit to blow.

Three A's, then:

*Aim*: to come face to face anew with the Lord who is calling us;

*Approach*: to expect in faith that God has a word for us;

*Attitude*: to see all as grace, all to be done grace-fully, spaciously, trustingly. Finally an exercise and then a verse of Scripture, to use or not to use, as you wish.

---

## QUIET TIME FOR REFLECTION

---

### *Application and Exercise*

The first exercise is a brief one: it is to apply (or begin to apply) to yourself the next of my alliterative groups, the great S's:

***Stillness Silence Solitude***

The exercise is simply to sit absolutely still for no less than five minutes, on your own, perhaps in your room before going to bed, and doing nothing except letting go of everything.

Although the exercise is 'simply' to sit absolutely still, of course we know it is not at all easy to sit still because most of us are too strung up, too busy, or in too much of a hurry to be able to remain totally still.

Slow down. That is what many of us need, literally and uncomplicatedly, to slow down. This exercise, performed in solitude, may also help to begin to quieten us, calm us, and to take us into inner silence where God's voice can be heard. So: Stillness, Silence, Solitude.

And the verse of Scripture? A most lovely one from Zephaniah 3:17, just the seven words,

*He will quiet you with His Love.*

What else but love can ultimately quieten us? What else can still us, still our storms, and silence our tumults? What else but love, *God's* Love? So as we slow down, settle, sit very still, we may repeat this verse, slowly, again and again, changing 'you' for 'me': so that 'He will quiet you with His Love', becomes 'He will quiet *me* with His Love'.

†

## Prayer

## Quiet me with Your Love

# 2
# THE ATTRACTIVENESS OF JESUS

Why choose the attractiveness of Jesus as a theme? I can answer best by sharing an experience of my own: in my early days at school God meant little to me. I did not dis-believe, did not call myself an atheist or an agnostic. It was just that many other things were more important and absorbing. To this day, I empathize very easily with the millions of people in this country who would say much the same: not active unbelief, but living with very little practical reference to the Author and Giver of Life.

Then one day, unexpectedly, the person of Jesus came alive for me. I cannot find any other way to express it. The person of Jesus came alive for me, as a presence, as an attraction, as a power; as a giver of peace and sense of coherence, as warmth, as a centre, and supremely real, the most real thing I knew. No doubt, psychological factors played a part. I have looked into these, and would accept that they did play a part, but only as the medium, a means by which something infinitely greater was given. For the soul or psyche has to be reached via the psychological channels. What I knew for certain, and knew instantly, and even more so after sixty years of testing, was that what I had been given was 'for real' and that it had come, so to speak, 'from beyond'. Jesus led me to God, absolutely straight to God, with no deviation: straight to the one He called 'Father', the source of all that is, infinitely beyond us, and yet most intimately present to us; transcendent and immanent. Steadily, steadily, the person of Jesus was acting in me like a magnet, a tremendous attraction drawing me into becoming a disciple.

I did not know then the Eastern Orthodox description of Jesus as 'the undistorted image of God', based on texts such as 2 Corinthians 4:4, 'the Gospel of the glory of Christ who is the image of God'; Colossians 1:13–15: 'He has rescued us from the power of darkness and transferred us into the kingdom of his beloved Son ... He is the image of the invisible God'; and 2 Corinthians 3:14–18:

> ... that same veil is still there, since only in Christ is it set aside. ... but when one turns to the Lord, the veil is removed. Now the Lord is the Spirit, and where the Spirit of the Lord is, there is freedom. And all of us, with unveiled faces, seeing the glory of the Lord as though reflected in a mirror, are being transformed into the same image from one degree of glory to another; for this comes from the Lord, the Spirit.

Ever since I came upon this description of Jesus as the undistorted image of God it has been my favourite statement of belief about Jesus in his relation to God. I believe in what it says, and I believe in the mysterious attractiveness of Jesus drawing everyone everywhere, without distinction, to God. All over the world, and in the most unexpected places, the signs appear of His attractive power: in films, in the theatre, in musicals, in popular songs, in novels, on the radio, on television ... there seems to be no getting away from this Person, who puzzles and yet attracts the world. Not, of course, that He is always presented without distortion—far from it—but that His image is somehow inescapable, even when rejected.

More specifically, I believe in the Community of Faith, the Church, that has been engendered by the Image; and in the word and sacraments that communicate the Image; and in the Holy Spirit who works to correct any distortions of God of which the Church and the preaching of the Word may be guilty. I mean that it is always the Holy Spirit who, despite fallen human errors and distortions, succeeds in conveying to us the

Spirit of *life*, the risen life of Christ—the actual life of God, revealing the Resurrection.

I have put my cards on the table like this so that you may understand better what lies behind the theme of this retreat; so that you may be able to enter into it, as the Spirit may lead you. I propose that we take the image of Jesus in its various aspects as our focus.

*Eikon* (Εικον from the Greek Testament) gives us the modern word icon. The huge popularity of icons, and the world trade in them is another sign of Jesus's attractive power. An icon is a focus, a focal point for the eyes, and for the eyes of the heart. An icon has a power of attraction, it has the power to transform those who focus on it. We may or may not use an icon in prayer, but in our lives we should similarly, each and every way, 'turn to the Lord'—this means facing Him—and face to face, to surrender ourselves to the request of His Love.

There is another symbol to which Scripture bids us turn, more universal than the icon: the symbol of the Cross. 'And I, when I am lifted up from the earth, will draw all people to myself' (John 12:32). Christ crucified is, strange though it may be, supremely attractive. So people all down the ages have found, although my experience is that we may have to live for a while, perhaps a long while, with the un-attractiveness of the Cross before its attractiveness unfolds. We may need to be honest and admit that Jesus himself is, at times, unattractive to us for various reasons, turning us away, turning us off. We may have to wait until, again, He becomes the focus that draws us. This applies to the early stages of retreat: we need to be patient, and honest with ourselves and with God. So let us meditate on Jesus in the spirit of honesty, and be open to His attractiveness.

## QUIET TIME FOR REFLECTION

## *Application*

There is a particularly appropriate passage for this: Mark 6:30–32. It is appropriate because it tells of disciples drawn back to be with Jesus after a time away on mission. In the New English Bible and Revised English Bible, three words appear in this passage beginning with the letter R—yes, another alliteration—and each of these words supplies us with a useful guideline. You will spot them easily:

> The Apostles re-joined Jesus and reported to him all that they had done and taught. He said to them, "Come away with me, by yourselves, to a deserted place and rest for a while." For people continued to come and go in great numbers, and they had no time even to eat. And so they went off by themselves in a boat to a deserted place.

The key words are *Re-join, Report, Rest.*

### *Re-join*

For the first disciples this meant literally coming back to Jesus after He had sent them out in mission. They came back to Him at a time of mounting crisis: St Mark places this return to Jesus between the Beheading of John the Baptist and the growing sense of opposition to Jesus on the one hand, and on the other the second half of the Gospel, the sense of catastrophe imminent, and the Passion narrative. For us, as we meditate today, what does 're-join' mean?

We have 'been away' in the sense of work, of active ministry, of retirement, and always finding we have so many things to attend to. Now, as we stop and give ourselves time to consider our faith and God, we have a chance to draw nearer to Him who calls us. Is there any other sense in which we need to 're-join Him'?

Has there been, for example, any 'wandering away' any 'straying' like the people of God in the wilderness? Even if there has been no outright disobedience to God, has there been any wavering or more subtle deviation from what we know in our hearts to be right? So is there any need to return and re-join Jesus, meaning to turn round in the right direction, and turn to Him? In short, is there any need of repentance, either from deliberate sin, or from a Sunday-only kind of half-hearted discipleship?

If so, we know that we need to deal with it straight away and straightforwardly; to make an Act of Repentance in some fashion, just as soon as we are honestly able to do so.

*Report*

Jesus wanted to know how the disciples had been getting on. He wanted to hear it from their own lips, face to face, in a group together and perhaps singly, privately. How does this apply to us?

I believe this applies directly: We are to believe that Christ is really interested in what we have been doing, really keen to hear from us, what is happening to us, what is on our minds, what is happy, what is unhappy. 'He knows it already', we may say. Yes, but the telling to Him really matters. One reason is that we often begin to notice more things in the telling. We sometimes get a fresh perspective on our private story in the course of telling it to someone else; so it is with Christ. How is our life and ministry going, no matter what that 'ministry' may be? Is there any weariness or sense of discomfort? Is there any sense of bewilderment over the direction our life is taking? Is there any oppressive tension between maintenance and mission? Any corrosion of spirit, like cynicism or scepticism? Any pain in personal relationships? Are there any successes to report? Any joys in ministry, signs of growth? Any growing assurance that God is real?

These are some of the things we can report on, and perhaps write down as part of this exercise, when we re-join Jesus and open our hearts to Him. 'Open our griefs', is what the 1662 Prayer Book says of confession. Let us open our joys as well.

*Rest*

For the disciples, as for us, the call to rest has a literal meaning. Physical rest is part of God's provision for our well-being. The deeper meaning is that our hearts (which also means our whole being) find rest in obedience to God: 'In His will is our peace'.[1] This is the 'Sabbath Rest' which remains for the People of God as the Bible means it: the place where, in obedience, God draws us into wholeness. Like a magnet drawing fragments of metal into unity, so the pieces of the divided self come together to rest in God.

### *Exercise*

Use the three Rs as 'pegs' on which to hang thoughts for prayer:

*Re-join*: penitence and reunion;
*Report*: tell Him all about it;
*Rest*: as if you were sitting on a beach by the seaside, basking in the sunshine of God's Love.

†

### Prayer

*May God guide us and keep us; may He show us the light of His countenance and give us His peace.*

[1] Dante Alighieri, *The Divine Comedy, Paradiso* III, 85. 'E'n la sua volontade è nostra pace'.

# 3
# THE ENERGY OF JESUS

St Paul says in Colossians 1:29, 'For this I toil and struggle with all the energy that he powerfully inspires within me.' He is talking about his pastoral ministry, his teaching and preaching, the energy and power of Christ: evidently this was common currency in the early Christian communities, that Jesus was a man of energy. St Paul here uses two Greek words to make his point: ἐνέργειαν (*energeian*) for the energy and δυνάμει (*dynamei* or dynamite!) for the power of Christ. Both words appear again and again in the New Testament, which is hardly surprising. This is the Jesus who, in about three years, started a movement that turned the world upside down, and whose arresting impact is felt two thousand years later with no diminution of power. The Jesus whose redemptive energy in his ministry evidently leapt out to everyone in need whom He met. The Jesus of 'Go and tell John what you have seen and heard: the blind receive their sight, the lame walk, the lepers are cleansed, the deaf hear, the dead are raised, the poor have good news brought to them.' (Luke 7:22); the Jesus who promised, and gave at Pentecost, the spirit and power to all disciples ready to carry on His ministry. No wonder the *energy* of Jesus is spoken of as it is in the New Testament: 'What is the immeasurable greatness of his power for us who believe', exclaimed the writer to the Ephesians (Eph. 1:19).

These are the resources available, constantly available, to all who draw upon them. 'Of this gospel', St Paul goes on, 'I have become a servant according to the gift of God's grace that was given me by the working of his power.' (Eph. 3:7).

What exactly do I mean, do I understand, by the 'energy' of Jesus? I do not see it as temperamental energy. I do not see in Him the least sign of temperamental compulsion, still less of temperamental frenzy. Most of us know what a lather people can get into when they are driven by inward compulsions of a neurotic kind: there is no place for them, they cannot rest, often they cannot stop.

The French Catholic philosopher Jacques Maritain (1882–1973) once drew the distinction I am making, when writing about Martin Luther. Maritain saw in Luther (whether rightly or wrongly) 'the energy of a temperament', a driven man, driven by inward conflicts not resolved.[2] He did not see in Luther 'the energy of a soul', as he put it, a soul at peace, and infused/energized without hindrance by the Holy Spirit.

Here lies the clue to understanding the energy of Jesus. There is a huge difference between the turbulent energy of a confused personality (confused, and confusing to others), and the pure energy of the Holy Spirit purely received by a person whom Christ is purifying. By 'purely received', I mean received without hindrance, without distortions, without manipulating the energy to egocentric ends.

In the unpeaceful turbulence of a confused person can be seen a distorted energy of God. In the pure energy of the Holy Spirit can be seen the beginnings, at least, of the undistorted image. So the divine energy in Jesus, seen in every penitent Christian who is being purified, is shown to be pure; not wasted, not ill-directed nor diluted, but governed by the Love that is pure, purely seeking the total well-being of everyone it meets. From the impact of this, the divine energy, comes Peace.

So this is not a destructive kind of power, not a steamrolling sort of energy. It is the power of Christ strangely made

---

[2] Jacques Maritain, *Three Reformers: Luther, Descartes, Rousseau* (Kennikat Press, 1970), 27.

perfect in weakness: the power of the Cross. Experience proves time and time again, paradoxical though it may be, that 'when I am weak, then I am strong' (2 Cor. 12:10). It is the power of the risen life that comes to our aid; the power that fills the 'Easter People'. It brings us, when we use it, the energy to start again, to return to our task, to resume prayer, to stop wasting what God has given us.

So, in this aspect of the undistorted image of God in Jesus, we come face to face with our Saviour, who can revitalize us in just those areas where we need it.

---

QUIET TIME FOR REFLECTION

---

## *Application*

I think it is important for us to recognize that the divine energy we are meditating on can be found throughout Creation. God is 'immanent' within His creation as well as outside it, or 'transcendent'.

In the 1960's we planted two young chestnut trees. For about five years they both grew up, straight and strong and splendid. Then one stormy night a violent south-westerly gale blew up. It snapped off the southern chestnut almost half way up, and left it looking derelict; but it left the other tree untouched. A pitiful sight: I thought it would all be over with the broken tree, and for about another five years that is exactly how it looked. But then one day I saw something appearing: it was a resurgence of life within the tree. Months went by, and more signs of life appeared, until at last it became clear that the tree had not only survived, but had reshaped itself. Rebuilding itself into a new beauty, not as tall as it might otherwise have been, but very beautiful. There is something else too: the tree that had suffered so much was now much thicker in the trunk and stronger than the one that had not suffered.

The creative energy of God, the immanent power of God, was in both trees, for their glory. This good energy, the 'flow' of life itself, became re-creative, redemptive, when the need arose. By the same token, when we go *with* the grain of life and not against it, we discover it contains the power of re-creation. We may also observe that those who have never been in trouble may not develop the same strength, in the end, as those who have.

Thus the divine energy is present throughout creation. It is available to us everywhere, through thousands of different channels of refreshment. All life is sacramental. However, the divine energy must not be wasted. What is it that wastes the energy? Principally two things: sin and fear. Sin because it wastes energy on things that can never satisfy us: 'false gods'. It is silly and self-destructive. 'Foolish' is the word Jesus uses for sin. Fear, because fear can soak up so much nervous energy.

The exercise I am going to suggest in this chapter, to consolidate this meeting with Jesus, is the aspect of energy. Concentrate on fear. In order to detect it, bring it out into the open of your own awareness and then combat it 'head on' in the Name of Jesus. It is not much use vaguely thinking about fear, as if it were a kind of choking fog (though it is!). we need to be specific: what precisely am I afraid of? Why am I afraid? What exactly am I wasting energy on?

So the exercise is to use a check-list for ourselves in the presence of Christ, in prayer, in order to spot the danger areas. I acknowledge my debt to the Anglican priest, author and spiritual director, Reginald Somerset Ward (1881–1962) in creating this list:

*Fear of inadequacy*: 'I haven't got what it takes so I had better not risk it'; either playing safe or bombastic talk; over-pushing, boasting, exaggerating; 'cover-up' behaviour.

*Fear of failure*: a further stage of the above. To try to avoid the pain of failure we put on masks to impress; we twist ourselves into unnatural shapes, distort ourselves; spoil the image with hollowness resulting.

*Fear of getting hurt*: of being blamed, of guilt and recrimination. 'Conscience can make cowards of us all'[3] therefore, make excuses, tell lies, shift blame.

*Fear of insecurity*: of losing someone's love, of rejection by my group, my congregation, my friends', of losing social reputation. Tricks for self-protection include going into a shell, or the opposite: coming out fighting, clinging, grasping.

*Fear of contact, or getting too close*: of intimacy in relationships, exposure, sexuality, keeping a safe distance. This has to be handled with self-knowledge.

*Fear of sickness, failing power, death, of dependence*: difficulty with entrusting oneself to others and finally letting go: avoiding thoughts of ageing or death, trying to stay young; hypochondria.

All these are possible forms of fear, and each one (if not dealt with) can soak up energy wastefully in suppressing it.

## *Exercise*

To detect and identify any fear(s) and write them down.

To bring them out, named, to Jesus our Saviour to tell Him.

To set to work with a daily act of counter attack, in the *power of the Spirit* to challenge my fear—go through the 'minefield' it represents—and trust the outcome to God.

[3] *Hamlet*, Act 3, sc. iv.

†

Prayer

*May the Holy Spirit give us*
*courage to face the truth about ourselves,*
*insight into our state, and*
*wisdom to see how to go forward,*
*in Christ's Name.*

# 4
# THE GENTLENESS AND FIERCENESS OF JESUS

## *Gentleness*

It seems to have been generally understood in the early days that Jesus was gentle. The Man of Energy was also the Man of Tenderness. So, for instance, St Paul wrote as from common ground in 2 Corinthians 10:1 'I myself, Paul, appeal to you by the meekness and gentleness of Christ'. The same Greek word for gentle is used by St Matthew in 11:28–30, presenting the great saying that is so apt for a retreat:

> Come to me, all you that are weary and are carrying heavy burdens, and I will give you rest. Take my yoke upon you, and learn from me; for I am gentle and humble in heart, and you will find rest for your souls.

We come to Jesus to learn from Him. To learn what? To learn whatever we may need to learn at this stage in our lives. We find in Him a gentle teacher. He may challenge us, He may be firm, even stern, with us, but He will measure His words to our capacity, and He will leave us in the end, not in turmoil or confusion, but in peace.

What is meant here by this word ἐπιεικείας (*epieikeias*), translated 'gentleness'? It is an interesting word in the original. As a verb, it means many things:

To calm a person or an animal—think of someone who knows how to do it: approaching a frightened horse, gently but firmly, with no haste, and finally slipping the harness over its head, the harness representing the yoke of which Jesus speaks;

To soothe—for example, to soothe a sore place;

To soften and make more flexible what is rigid—as in the hymn to the Holy Spirit: 'What is rigid gently bend; what is frozen, warmly tend'.[4] Warmth, personal warmth, and gentleness go together: 'the fruit of the Spirit is love, joy, peace, patience, kindness, generosity, faithfulness, gentleness, and self-control.' (Gal. 5:22–3). The Spirit of Jesus shows in the Christian's gentleness.

How do we, now, directly experience the gentleness of Jesus? We know it when, through Him, we receive forgiveness for our sins, forgiveness and reconciliation. We know it on Good Friday and Easter Day if we catch a fresh glimpse of the truth that 'in His hands He gently bears us, rescues us from all our foes' and that we are 'Ransomed, healed, restored, forgiven'.[5] It is, I find, sinners who know they are forgiven who have the most profound sense of God's gentleness and who can be gentle with others.

Again, we have His touch, gentle and firm, when (in prayer, perhaps) the Holy Spirit calms us and pulls us together just when we are in danger of falling apart. At such moments, we can catch sight of the face of the ultimate reality, for 'Whoever has seen me has seen the Father', said Jesus (John 14:9). Jesus reveals to us without distinction, in word and action, the heart of God. It proves to be a heart of tenderness, sensitivity, gentleness.

---

[4] From the hymn 'Come, thou Holy Paraclete', *English Hymnal,* 155; reproduced below, p. 33.

[5] 'Praise my soul the King of Heaven', *New English Hymnal,* 436.

At the same time, intertwined with this understanding of Jesus in the Gospels, is the evidence of the fierceness of Jesus. This evidence would surely have been suppressed if the Gospel writers had been trying to attract converts by presenting nothing but a superficial gentleness. This would be treacle or soft soap, supplied for religious self-indulgence. But not a bit of it: they transmitted a tradition which showed that at times Jesus was fierce. In St Matthew, for example, we find a most extraordinary instance of this: in 21:5 comes one of the most important verses in the New Testament about Jesus' gentleness, where Jesus was riding into Jerusalem on a donkey, and St Matthew comments on it by quoting the prophecy of Zephaniah: 'See, your king comes to you, gentle and riding on a donkey' (in the NIV translation). Yet seven verses later St Matthew says that gentle Jesus went into the Temple and drove out (ἐξέβαλεν [*exebalen*], the word is fierce, whatever precisely Jesus did) all who were buying and selling, and upset (κατέστρεψεν [*katestrepsen*] this word is even fiercer) the tables of the money-changers.

How fiercely, too, Jesus rebuked Peter: 'Get behind me, Satan' (Matt. 16:23 and Mark 8:33); rebuked all his disciples, 'indignantly' for trying to stop children coming to Him; how fiercely He exploded at unbelief, and at consequent impotence in ministry! 'What an unbelieving generation', He cried out. What fierce language He used when He found shams and pretences or cover-ups or self-satisfaction and wilful blindness, or the religious exploitation of the 'little ones' who could easily be manipulated. 'woe to you, scribes and Pharisees, hypocrites!' (Matt. 23:13), you blind guides, blind fools, snakes, vipers brood. Passion is in these words, and an explosive force of Passion.

We might make matters easier for ourselves if we enquired into this evidence and tried to explain it away, but if we were to do so, we would miss a vital aspect of the image of God in Jesus. For the gentleness, and fierceness of Jesus may appear to be contradictory, but they are in fact complementary. They are two sides of the same coin. The coin is love, pure love, passionate and strong, love.

You must have seen this reflected in good parents who love their children tenderly, and who do not allow their children to get away with things that are harmful. God does not allow us to get away with things: sooner or later He pulls us up, and the tug on the reins may be fierce if it needs to be. God's love for us, seen in Jesus, is a blazing passion for our salvation, that we may be untwisted, undistorted, healed and made happy.

## QUIET TIME FOR REFLECTION

### *Application*

How important it is that Christian communities, parishes, churches, be marked by gentleness! Put on garments that suit God's beloved people says St Paul in Colossians 3:12, 'clothe yourselves with compassion, kindness, humility, meekness, and patience'. How important that we should be gentle! 'But as for you, ... pursue righteousness, godliness, faith, love, endurance, gentleness' (1 Tim. 6:11). Strong gentleness, not soft, is clearly indicated here, because in the same breath as we are told to pursue gentleness, we are told to pursue justice and integrity.

A few years ago, a man approaching middle age began a long search for a spiritual home. He told me that he was looking for a Christian community—or 'ecclesial community'—a church, as he put it, marked by three characteristics: honesty, gentleness and freedom. I should never forget his three chosen words: honesty, gentleness and freedom. And I thank God that he was able to find those things within the Anglican tradition. He now ministers as a priest.

How, then, can the gentleness of Jesus be manifest in us? First, all the signs are that in Jesus the power of body and soul were unified. They were brought together by a common purpose: to glorify God. In modern language, Jesus was integrated, though the term sounds rather too cold, for Jesus was passionate but not cold. He was clearly moved, and deeply so, by feelings of joy, delight, and compassion, as well as by indignation and outrage. He allowed his strong feelings to have their place and they were given their head, without distortion.

Second, we know that we cannot be gentle with others if we are not at peace with ourselves. We cannot be gentle with others if we are warring against ourselves, or against some part of ourselves, a part of which perhaps we do not approve. We cannot be gentle with others if we are rejecting and trying to crush a part of ourselves, as if to extinguish it. The despised parts of our personality, our body and soul, will not be extinguished: they cannot be. They will not even lie down and keep quiet; they persist as sources of severe disturbance. They will break out, sooner or later, in some type of violence, in deed or in speech.

The clue to gentleness lies in the way we respond to the feelings that arise in us from the body and soul; positive and negative feelings such as desire (desire is positive in being full of good potential); or negative feelings such as resentment, frustration, adversity. In every feeling is a message for us, and a call to constructive response. The title of a book published in France in the 1950s has always stayed with me: it was *My Friends the Senses*.[6] It means to us (and this is the clue to gentleness) that we should keep in touch with our senses as we would with our friends. That we should not be afraid of them, but regard them as allies. They can help us in our pilgrimage; to enjoy sights,

[6] Charles Damian Boulogne, *My Friends the Senses*, trans. Jane Howes (Burns & Oates, 1954).

sounds, flavours and touch is not separate from prayer or from loving God and enjoying Him for ever, it is an integral part of it. So the clue to gentleness lies in being in touch with our emotions and respecting them, for only by accepting what I am (feelings and all) can I be brought into inner harmony and peace. Then the gentleness of real strength will appear of its own accord. St Francis de Sales said, 'Nothing is so strong as gentleness; nothing is so loving and gentle as strength'.[7]

### *Exercise*

Come before God in prayer. Ask for the Holy Spirit's light. Put three questions to yourself and write down notes for an answer:

Is there anyone in my life with whom I am not being gentle, whether in my thoughts or words or deeds? Press the question, *why*?

Is there anything about myself that I am hating, or refusing to acknowledge? Being violent about?

Is there anything I can do to develop my 'friendship with my senses', to develop my use of them in happy directions? Noticing more; enjoying more.

†

### Prayer

*May Christ lead us to see in ourselves*
*what He wants us to see.*
*May He heal us and give us His peace.*

[7] C. F. Kelly, ed., *The Spiritual Maxims of St. Francis de Sales* (Longmans Green, 1954), 124.

# 5
# THE CONFIDENCE OF JESUS

Was there ever a time when Jesus was not confident? Yes, according to St Mark, there was. It happened in the Garden of Gethsemane where dismay came over him. Amazement at the turn of events was part of it, also shock and horror at what was happening. He was staggered by it and his confidence came under attack.

I have studied what some of the commentators say about this passage in St Mark 14:32–6, and find agreement. 'So far from sailing serenely through his trials like some superior being unconcerned with this world, Jesus is almost dead with distress'.[8] 'The episode is so unexpected that it is difficult to see how (as some have tried to make out) it could have been invented by the Church.'[9] It was indeed unexpected, and this is because, up to that moment, the Gospels present Jesus as entirely confident. Confident in God: His words, His deeds, His teaching (not as the scribes, but as one with authority), and especially His proclamation of the kingdom of God. It has come, and it is coming in fullness. This is the dawn (so He answered with assurance), the dawn of this coming Age—'the kingdom of God has come to you' (Matt. 12:28).

Does the exception in the Garden of Gethsemane prove the rule? It certainly highlights it, but it is precious because it brings

---

[8] C. F. D Moule, *The Gospel According to Mark* (Cambridge University Press, 1965), 117.

[9] Anthony Harvey, *A Companion to the New Testament* (Cambridge University Press, 2004), 196.

Jesus close to us, and us to Him, in knowing what it is like to have our confidence shaken. Jesus is close also to Christians such as the martyrs, prisoners, hostages and the tortured ones, who cry out to God in the horror and dismay that overtake them, when the foundations of their faith are shaken.

There is something else about the confidence of Jesus revealed in the Gospels: it is that the fullness of confidence lay for Him on the other side of the resurrection. The Risen Christ came among the Apostles and said, 'Peace be with you' (Luke 23:36); 'Do not be afraid' (Matt. 28:10); 'All authority in heaven and on earth has been given to me.' (Matt. 28:18); 'I am with you always, to the end of the age.' (Matt. 28:20). After the Resurrection, what inspired confidence in the disciples was His interpretation of Scripture: 'Then he opened their minds to understand the Scriptures' (Luke 24:45). That is to say He interpreted what was actually happening to them in such a way that their confidence was restored and renewed by their new insight into the events that had so crushed them.

For us, too, it can happen that we are saved from despondency by coming to see through counselling the correct interpretation of what is happening to us; the place of our suffering in God's saving work for us. For us, too, the fullness of confidence lies on the other side of the Cross, in resurrection. Most of us do not know fullness until we have experienced emptiness: the emptiness of weakness, of being drained out, of being knocked out, of being humiliated, or, in Pauline terms, of being buried with Christ and raised with Him 'in newness of life' (Rom. 6:4). When we have been through this cycle a good many times confidence in God develops. Then we know, and know so much more confidently, the power of the risen life. The victory of the Cross comes true in our experience. Resurrection is revealed not as a thing, but as Him: the presence, the ever-new, ever-renewing presence of Christ, Crucified and Risen.

## *Application*

Is the Church of England in a state of crisis? If it is, how does this affect our confidence? I offer a passage here that captures the true spirit of Christian confidence:

> The Church is always in a crisis and always will be. Difficulties, limitations, insoluble problems, want of men and money, a menacing outlook, endless misunderstandings and misrepresentations—we have not just to do our work in spite of these things; they are precisely the conditions required for the doing of it, and the proofs that we are at grips with our real task. If we are 'pressed', it means that we are pressing others, for all pressure is reciprocal; so far from its 'straightening us', it means that our influence is growing wider. If we are 'perplexed' by our intellectual and practical problems, it means that we are facing them; those who refuse to face them suffer from no perplexity.[10]

The author concludes: 'Always with more work than we can do, with harder problems than we can solve, never seeing how the work is going to be done, and yet, when the time comes, doing it.'

Confidence of this quality is bound up with an even more fundamental matter and that is belief in Divine Providence. I value highly the classic work by Jean-Pierre de Caussade, *Self-abandonment to the Divine Providence*, and the related practice of *The Sacrament of the Present Moment*.[11] A Bishop of St Helena,

[10] Henry Leighton Goudge, *The Mind of St Paul: As Illustrated by His Second Epistle to the Corinthians* (E. Arnold, 1911), 103.

[11] *Self-abandonment to the Divine Providence,* English translation of the tenth French Edition, ed. Fr H. Ramière SJ (Lulu.com, 2018); *The Sacrament of the Present Moment,* trans. Kitty Muggeridge (Harper Collins, 1989).

while dying from cancer, once wrote to me that he was finding, in his present crisis, that de Caussade's *The Sacrament of the Present Moment* is his spiritual mainstay, and gives him a 'splendid sense of peace'. In other words, grace is found precisely in the contents of each moment in one's life.

Confidence and self-abandonment to the Divine Providence … Yes, but suppose our belief in Divine Providence has been shaken, not only by personal tragedies, but also by the battering in the Church that the doctrine of Divine Providence has taken. Dietrich Bonhoeffer in his Nazi prison-cell had to re-think the doctrine, and Christian writers have been wrestling with it (as have Jewish writers since the Holocaust) ever since.

### *What are we to believe?*

There are, I believe two extremes: one is that God has us as puppets on a string so that everything is determined; the other is that God does nothing, and is effectively absent, so as to leave us free and totally responsible—and in particular that He is not 'interventionist', sometimes intervening, sometimes leaving us to ourselves.

### *What is the truth?*

I do not think we can abdicate responsibility and say that it is all beyond us, too mysterious for us. It is mysterious—God does work in a mysterious way—but we are sure to have in our thoughts, whether consciously or unconsciously, a model of God's presence or absence in human affairs. It will make a big difference to our level of confidence in practice, and to the way we face the future, if we review our beliefs or models, and press home in ourselves the question: is it true? Even if our answer is provisional, it is better than an evasion, better than a kind of spiritual smudge.

The Bible gives a marvellous account in story-form of the operation of Divine Providence in the story of Joseph in Genesis Chapter 37. His brothers had sold him into slavery; when, much later, they find him still alive and in high office in Egypt as Pharaoh's right-hand man, they are terrified. But Joseph calms them gently, and gives them a different interpretation of events. The key verses are from Genesis 45:4–8:

> He said, "I am your brother, Joseph, whom you sold into Egypt. And now do not be distressed, or angry with yourselves, because you sold me here; for God sent me before you to preserve life. For the famine has been in the land these two years; and there are five more years in which there will be neither ploughing nor harvest. God sent me before you to preserve for you a remnant on earth, and to keep alive for you many survivors. So it was not you who sent me here, but God ..."

To Joseph it was clear, but of course it was not to everyone, for the brothers were responsible for a brutal act. However, the eye of faith saw in it more than that. The eye of faith saw God at work to bring good out of evil. "Even though you intended to do harm to me, God intended it for good" (Gen 50:20). The story of Genesis is quite a sophisticated statement of belief in Divine Providence. It is reflected in Romans 8:28: 'We know that all things work together for good for those who love God, who are called according to his purpose.' If I had to put this concept in a single sentence, it would be this: 'Not everything that happens is God's direct will, but God is at work to fulfil His will in every situation.'

What appeals to me especially in this is trust. It is not a static, but a dynamic view of providence; not something fixed but something being worked out from moment to moment by the creative energy of God. It sees the Holy Spirit as continuously living and active, 'like a two-edged sword' (Rev. 1:16). In this I can find confidence, for life and for death, for facing whatever may come.

## *For prayer time*

Before suggesting an Exercise, I want to tell you a modern and true story that also illustrates this view of providence. An actor with the Royal Shakespeare Company at Stratford who was playing Hamlet, went for a walk in the countryside near the town. He came upon two woodsmen who were cutting branches from a hedge. He asked them what they were doing. One of them replied: "Well, it's like this: I rough-hews them, and he shapes their ends." The actor walked on and at once remembered that he was going to say on stage that night: 'There's a divinity that shapes our ends, rough-hew them how we will'.[12]

I found that study in an autobiography called *Rough Hewing* by Colin Trevor, a Roman Catholic priest who became Anglican.[13] In it he raises the intricate combination of the human and the Divine in his life. He concludes that on his side, he had done a lot of 'rough-hewing' (hacking away at things), and yet through it all God had shaped the course of his life (inner and outer) to its destined purpose.

## *Exercise*

An affirmation of faith: write down a statement of what you believe in your heart about Divine Providence, in the world and in your life. Affirm your faith in word and gesture, with upraised hands: 'Lord, I believe ...'

Into that context, place your present situation: problems, hopes, concerns, in an act of trust and surrender: in word, gesture, open hands and abandon.

---

[12] *Hamlet,* Act 5, sc. ii.

[13] Colin Trevor, *Rough Hewing: A Marriage and a Ministry* (Churchman, 1990).

†

Prayer

May the Lord direct your hearts
into the love of God and into the
steadfastness of Christ.
(2 Thess. 3:5)

# 6
# THE STEADFASTNESS OF JESUS

*May the Lord direct your hearts into the love of God and into the steadfastness of Christ.*

What a beautiful prayer this is from 2 Thessalonians 3:5. 'Lord' here is, I believe, the Holy Spirit. The Spirit directs, guides, enables; is our Spiritual Director. You do not have to make a journey to see Him, He is always available, always reliable.

'Direct ... into the love of God', in other words into a deepened sense that God loves us; 'Into' like moving into a new home: our Baptismal home; into the steadfastness of Christ, into another aspect of the character of Jesus commonly understood in the early Church. It means endurance and holding to one course all through life and when death approaches, as when Jesus steadfastly 'set his face to go to Jerusalem' (Luke 9:51).

In this also Jesus is the undistorted image of God. He shows us the steadfast love of God spoken of by the Prophets,

> I will recount the gracious deeds of the Lord,
> the praiseworthy acts of the Lord,
> because of all that the Lord has done for us,
> and the great favour to the house of Israel
> that he has shown them according to his mercy,
> according to the abundance of his steadfast love.

(Is. 63:7)

Notice how important it is that these two key words of our prayer-text go together, *steadfastness* and *love*. Steadfastness on its own could be merely a gritting of the teeth, a dogged determination, even an obstinacy: an unlovely thing.

*Steadfastness without love is cold*
*Steadfastness with love is Christ-like.*

St Boniface was martyred on 5 June 755 at Dokkum, when a band of Frisians attacked him while he was reading Scripture to newly converted Christians on Pentecost Sunday. What made the martyrdom of St Boniface a burning and a shining light was the love that led him to it. St Boniface did not have to go on that last missionary journey to Frisia. He was 74 years old by then; he could have remained simply as Archbishop of Mainz and retired with great honour. But the love of Christ constrained him and he set off again to preach the Gospel. When a huge hostile force attacked him and all his clergy he was steadfast to the end, forbidding the young priests to fight as they wanted to: 'Do not render evil for evil', he said. They were nearly all killed, but the steadfast love, a loving steadfastness, bore fruit: many conversions to Christ followed.

From middle age onwards, we may keep going in discipleship, in ministry, and personal discipline under the yoke of Christ. But there is a danger that although we may carry on our duties in public and in private, although we may be outwardly steadfast, we may begin to lose the heart of love in them. For example, we may go on saying the Offices a.m. and p.m., which is fine and important, but that is not an end in itself. Praying from the heart is what keeps us close to Jesus. The danger in later years is that steadfastness may become separated from love.

Is our time of prayer directing us, drawing us, into a deeper sense of God's love, deeper into a personal relationship with God? If it is not then we should think again about our way of praying. What else can we do to keep love and steadfastness together? We cannot force ourselves to have a deepened sense of God's love, but we can hold ourselves open to receiving it.

## QUIET TIME FOR REFLECTION

### *Exercise*

Hold yourself open to receive deeply into yourself a fresh sense of God's love.

†

### Prayer

*Let us see this moment as a foretaste of that Heavenly Banquet where we shall be together in the Communion of the Saints, and see God without distortion, face to face in glory, to whom be Glory and Praise for ever, Amen.*

# NOTES ON THE USE OF QUIET TIME

*Preparation*

Decide in advance on time and place: a minimum length of time, and find as private a place as possible. It may be a good idea to ask other people in your household not to disturb you. Turn off your computer and mobile phone.

Have paper and pencil handy; have a Bible to hand, and perhaps a picture or icon to look at if this helps you; settle down in the posture that suits you best, that may least distract you.

*Stillness*

Practise a few minutes of total stillness, by letting go of tensions. 'Be still, and know that I am God' (Ps. 46:10).

Practise a few minutes of calm, regular breathing. 'Breathe on me, Breath of God' (*Hymns Ancient and Modern*, no. 157).

Say (or sing) as a prayer the hymn, 'Come Thou holy Paraclete':

> Come, Thou holy Paraclete,
> And from Thy celestial seat
> Send Thy light and brilliancy:
>
> Father of the poor, draw near;
> Giver of all gifts, be here;
> Come, the soul's true radiancy.
>
> Come, of comforters the best,
> Of the soul the sweetest guest,
> Come in toil refreshingly.

Thou in labour rest most sweet,
Thou art shadow from the heat,
Comfort in adversity.

O Thou Light, most pure and blest,
Shine within the inmost breast
Of Thy faithful company.

Where Thou art not, man hath naught;
Every holy deed and thought
Comes from Thy divinity.

What is soilèd, make Thou pure;
What is wounded, work its cure;
What is parchèd, fructify;

What is rigid, gently bend;
What is frozen, warmly tend;
Strengthen what goes erringly.

Fill Thy faithful, who confide
In Thy power to guard and guide,
With Thy sevenfold mystery.

Here Thy grace and virtue send:
Grant salvation in the end,
And in heaven felicity.[14]

## *Lectio Divina*

Read slowly straight through a set passage from the Bible or one that you particularly wish to meditate upon. If you have no particular passage in mind I suggest one of the following. These passages are taken from the NRSV, but if you prefer a different translation, use your own.

[14] *English Hymnal*, no. 155. This version of the text is taken from *The Presbyterian Book of Praise* (Oxford University Press, 1915), no. 110.

# I

## *John 14: 16–26*

And I will ask the Father, and he will give you another Advocate, to be with you forever. This is the Spirit of truth, whom the world cannot receive, because it neither sees him nor knows him. You know him, because he abides with you, and he will be in you.

I will not leave you orphaned; I am coming to you. In a little while the world will no longer see me, but you will see me; because I live, you also will live. On that day you will know that I am in my Father, and you in me, and I in you. They who have my commandments and keep them are those who love me; and those who love me will be loved by my Father, and I will love them and reveal myself to them. Judas (not Iscariot) said to him, "Lord, how is it that you will reveal yourself to us, and not to the world?" Jesus answered him, "Those who love me will keep my word, and my Father will love them, and we will come to them and make our home with them. Whoever does not love me does not keep my words; and the word that you hear is not mine, but is from the Father who sent me."

I have said these things to you while I am still with you. But the Advocate, the Holy Spirit, whom the Father will send in my name, will teach you everything, and remind you of all that I have said to you.

# II

*John 15: 18–27*

If the world hates you, be aware that it hated me before it hated you. If you belonged to the world, the world would love you as its own. Because you do not belong to the world, but I have chosen you out of the world—therefore the world hates you. Remember the word that I said to you, "Servants are not greater than their master." If they persecuted me, they will persecute you; if they kept my word, they will keep yours also. But they will do all these things to you on account of my name, because they do not know him who sent me. If I had not come and spoken to them, they would not have sin; but now they have no excuse for their sin. Whoever hates me hates my Father also. If I had not done among them the works that no one else did, they would not have sin. But now they have seen and hated both me and my Father. It was to fulfill the word that is written in their law, 'They hated me without a cause.'

When the Advocate comes, whom I will send to you from the Father, the Spirit of truth who comes from the Father, he will testify on my behalf. You also are to testify because you have been with me from the beginning.

# III

*John 16: 1–15*

I have said these things to you to keep you from stumbling. They will put you out of the synagogues. Indeed, an hour is coming when those who kill you will think that by doing so they are offering worship to God. And they will do this because they have not known the Father or me. But I have said these things to you so that when their hour comes you may remember that I told you about them. I did not say these things to you from the beginning, because I was with you. But now I am going to him who sent me; yet none of you asks me, "Where are you going?" But because I have said these things to you, sorrow has filled your hearts. Nevertheless I tell you the truth: it is to your advantage that I go away, for if I do not go away, the Advocate will not come to you; but if I go, I will send him to you. And when he comes, he will prove the world wrong about sin and righteousness and judgment: about sin, because they do not believe in me; about righteousness, because I am going to the Father and you will see me no longer; about judgment, because the ruler of this world has been condemned.

I still have many things to say to you, but you cannot bear them now. When the Spirit of truth comes, he will guide you into all the truth; for he will not speak on his own, but will speak whatever he hears, and he will declare to you the things that are to come. He will glorify me, because he will take what is mine and declare it to you. All that the Father has is mine. For this reason I said that he will take what is mine and declare it to you.

# IV

*1 John 2: 1–2*

My little children, I am writing these things to you so that you may not sin. But if anyone does sin, we have an advocate with the Father, Jesus Christ the righteous; and he is the atoning sacrifice for our sins, and not for ours only but also for the sins of the whole world.

Go back over the passage: focus on a little at a time, and ask the Holy Spirit and yourself questions like, What does this mean? What did it mean to the writer? What does it mean to me now, in my life-situation, in my home, my work, my personal relationship with God? Is there any kind of message for me? Jot down any thoughts that may occur to you. Turn over in your heart the words of Scripture, to appreciate and gaze at them, as you might turn over in your hand a precious jewel.

*Generally*

Prayer is any movement of the heart towards God. So speak freely to God, let emotions flow if they want to, and express your feelings (whatever they may be) to the One who listens with love and compassion.

Jot down any conclusions, if any occur to you. Don't worry if nothing very much comes to mind.

*After*

Thank God for your quiet time, whatever it has been like.

†

## Other ways of entering Prayer

By examination of conscience: 'opening our griefs', and telling God what is wrong.

By examination of consciousness: unfolding in God's presence the contents of our emotions and pressing concerns, and speaking of them briefly; moving on from there to becoming more centred upon Him as the Spirit draws us.

By starting not where we are, but with somebody else's material (such as Scripture or a devotional text) and making it our own as the Spirit guides and makes relevant.

# SLG PRESS PUBLICATIONS

| | | |
|---|---|---|
| FP1 | *Prayer and the Life of Reconciliation* | Gilbert Shaw (1969) |
| FP2 | *Aloneness Not Loneliness* | Mother Mary Clare SLG (1969) |
| FP4 | *Intercession* | Mother Mary Clare SLG (1969) |
| FP8 | *Prayer: Extracts from the Teaching of Fr Gilbert Shaw* | Gilbert Shaw (1973) |
| FP12 | *Learning to Pray* | Mother Mary Clare SLG (1970) |
| FP15 | *Death, the Gateway to Life* | Gilbert Shaw (1971) |
| FP16 | *The Victory of the Cross* | Dumitru Stăniloae (1970) |
| FP26 | *The Message of Saint Seraphim* | Irina Gorainov (1974) |
| FP28 | *Julian of Norwich: Four Studies to Commemorate the Sixth Centenary of the Revelations of Divine Love* | Sr Benedicta Ward SLG, Sr Eileen Mary SLG, ed. A. M. Allchin (1973) |
| FP43 | *The Power of the Name: The Jesus Prayer in Orthodox Spirituality* | Kallistos Ware (1974) |
| FP46 | *Prayer and Contemplation* and *Distractions are for Healing* | Robert Llewelyn (1975) |
| FP48 | *The Wisdom of the Desert Fathers* | trans. Sr Benedicta Ward SLG (1975) |
| FP50 | *Letters of Saint Antony the Great* | trans. Derwas Chitty (1975, 2/2021) |
| FP54 | *From Loneliness to Solitude* | Roland Walls (1976) |
| FP55 | *Theology and Spirituality* | Andrew Louth (1976, rev. 1978) |
| FP61 | *Kabir: The Way of Love and Paradox* | Sr Rosemary SLG (1977) |
| FP62 | *Anselm of Canterbury: A Monastic Scholar* | Sr Benedicta Ward SLG (1973) |
| FP63 | *Evelyn Underhill, Anglican Mystic: Two Centenary Essays* | A. M. Allchin, Bp Michael Ramsey (2/1996) |
| FP67 | *Mary and the Mystery of the Incarnation: An Essay on the Mother of God in the Theology of Karl Barth* | Andrew Louth (1977) |
| FP68 | *Trinity and Incarnation in Anglican Tradition* | A. M. Allchin (1977) |
| FP70 | *Facing Depression* | Gonville ffrench-Beytagh (1978, 2/2020) |
| FP71 | *The Single Person* | Philip Welsh (1979) |
| FP72 | *The Letters of Ammonas, Successor of St Antony* | trans. Derwas Chitty (1979) |
| FP74 | *George Herbert, Priest and Poet* | Kenneth Mason (1980) |
| FP75 | *A Study of Wisdom: Three Tracts by the Author of The Cloud of Unknowing* | trans. Clifton Wolters (1980) |
| FP78 | *Silence in Prayer and Action* | Sr Edmée SLG (1981) |

FP81 *The Psalms: Prayer Book of the Bible*
Dietrich Bonhoeffer, trans. Sr Isabel SLG (1982)
FP82 *Prayer and Holiness* Dumitru Stăniloae (1982)
FP85 *Walter Hilton: Eight Chapters on Perfection and Angels' Song*
trans. Rosemary Dorward (1983)
FP88 *Creative Suffering* Iulia de Beausobre (1983)
FP90 *Bringing Forth Christ: Five Feasts of the Child Jesus by St Bonaventure*
trans. Eric Doyle OFM (1984)
FP92 *Gentleness in John of the Cross* Thomas Kane (1985)
FP93 *Prayer: The Work of the Spirit* Sr Edmée SLG (1985)
FP94 *Saint Gregory Nazianzen: Selected Poems* trans. John McGuckin (1986)
FP95 *The World of the Desert Fathers: Stories & Sayings from the Anonymous Series of the Apophthegmata Patrum* trans. Columba Stewart OSB (1986, 2/2020)
FP101 *Anglicanism: A Canterbury Essay* Kenneth Mason (1987)
FP104 *Growing Old with God* T. N. Rudd (1988, 2/2020)
FP105 *The Simplicity of Prayer: Extracts from the Teaching of Mother Mary Clare SLG*
Mother Mary Clare SLG (1988)
FP106 *Julian Reconsidered* Kenneth Leech, Sr Benedicta SLG (1988)
FP108 *The Unicorn: Meditations on the Love of God* Harry Galbraith Miller (1989)
FP109 *The Creativity of Diminishment* Sister Anke (1990)
FP111 *A Kind of Watershed: An Anglican Lay View of Sacramental Confession*
Christine North (1990)
FP116 *Jesus, the Living Lord* Bp Michael Ramsey (1992)
FP117 *The Spirituality of Saint Cuthbert* Sr Benedicta Ward SLG (1992)
FP120 *The Monastic Letters of St Athanasius the Great* trans. Leslie Barnard (1994)
FP122 *The Hidden Joy* Sr Jane SLG, ed. Dorothy Sutherland (1994)
FP123 *At the Lighting of the Lamps: Hymns of the Ancient Church*
trans. John McGuckin (1995)
FP124 *Prayer of the Heart: An Approach to Silent Prayer and Prayer in the Night*
Alexander Ryrie (1995, 3/2020)
FP125 *Whole Christ: The Spirituality of Ministry* Philip Seddon (1996)
FP127 *Apostolate and the Mirrors of Paradox*
Sydney Evans, ed. Andrew Linzey, Brian Horne (1996)
FP128 *The Wisdom of Saint Isaac the Syrian* Sebastian Brock (1997)
FP129 *Saint Thérèse of Lisieux: Her Relevance for Today* Sr Eileen Mary SLG (1997)
FP130 *Expectations: Five Addresses for Those Beginning Ministry*
Sr Edmée SLG (1997)
FP131 *Scenes from Animal Life: Fables for the Enneagram Types*
Waltraud Kirschke, trans. Sr Isabel SLG (1998)
FP132 *Praying the Word of God: The Use of Lectio Divina*
Charles Dumont OCSO (1999)
FP134 *The Hidden Way of Love: Jean-Pierre de Caussade's Spirituality of Abandonment* Barry Conaway (1999)

FP135 *Shepherd and Servant: The Spiritual Theology of Saint Dunstan* Douglas Dales (2000)
FP136 *Eternity and Time* Dumitru Stăniloae, trans. A. M. Allchin (2001)
FP137 *Pilgrimage of the Heart* Sr Benedicta Ward SLG (2001)
FP138 *Mixed Life* Walter Hilton, trans. Rosemary Dorward (2001)
FP140 *A Great Joy: Reflections on the Meaning of Christmas* Kenneth Mason (2001)
FP141 *Bede and the Psalter* Sr Benedicta Ward SLG (2002)
FP142 *Abhishiktananda: A Memoir of Dom Henri Le Saux* Murray Rogers, David Barton (2003)
FP143 *Friendship in God: The Encounter of Evelyn Underhill & Sorella Maria of Campello* A. M. Allchin (2003)
FP144 *Christian Imagination in Poetry and Polity: Some Anglican Voices from Temple to Herbert* Archbp Rowan Williams (2004)
FP145 *The Reflections of Abba Zosimas, Monk of the Palestinian Desert* trans. John Chryssavgis (2004)
FP146 *The Gift of Theology: The Trinitarian Vision of Ann Griffiths and Elizabeth of Dijon* A. M. Allchin (2005)
FP147 *Sacrifice and Spirit* Bp Michael Ramsey (2005)
FP148 *Saint John Cassian on Prayer* trans. A. M Casiday (2006)
FP149 *Hymns of Saint Ephrem the Syrian* trans. Mary Hansbury (2006)
FP150 *Suffering: Why all this Suffering? What Do I Do about It?* Reinhard Körner OCD, trans. Sr Avis Mary SLG (2006)
FP151 *A True Easter: The Synod of Whitby 664 AD* Sr Benedicta Ward SLG (2007)
FP152 *Prayer as Self-Offering* Alexander Ryrie (2007)
FP153 *From Perfection to the Elixir: How George Herbert Fashioned a Famous Poem* Ben de la Mare (2008)
FP154 *The Jesus Prayer: Gospel Soundings* Sr Pauline Margaret CHN (2008)
FP155 *Loving God Whatever: Through the Year with Sister Jane* Sister Jane SLG (2006)
FP156 *Prayer and Meditation for a Sleepless Night* SISTERS OF THE LOVE OF GOD (2/2009)
FP157 *Being There: Caring for the Bereaved* John Porter (2009)
FP158 *Learn to Be at Peace: The Practice of Stillness* Andrew Norman (2010)
FP159 *From Holy Week to Easter* George Pattison (2010)
FP160 *Strength in Weakness: The Scandal of the Cross* John W. Rogerson (2010)
FP161 *Augustine Baker: Frontiers of the Spirit* Victor de Waal (2010)
FP162 *Out of the Depths* Gonville ffrench-Beytagh; epilogue Wendy Robinson (2/2010)
FP163 *God and Darkness: A Carmelite Perspective* Gemma Hinricher OCD, trans. Sr Avis Mary SLG (2010)
FP164 *The Gift of Joy* Curtis Almquist SSJE (2011)
FP165 *'I Have Called You Friends': Suggestions for the Spiritual Life Based on the Farewell Discourses of Jesus* Reinhard Körner OCD (2012)
FP166 *Leisure* Mother Mary Clare SLG (2012)

| | | |
|---|---|---|
| FP167 | *Carmelite Ascent: An Introduction to St Teresa and St John of the Cross* | Mother Mary Clare SLG (rev. 2012) |
| FP168 | *Ann Griffiths and Her Writings* | Llewellyn Cumings (2012) |
| FP169 | *The Our Father* | Sr Benedicta Ward SLG (2012) |
| FP170 | *Exploring Silence* | Wendy Robinson (1974, 3/2013) |
| FP171 | *The Spiritual Wisdom of the Syriac Book of Steps* | Robert A Kitchen (2013) |
| FP172 | *The Prayer of Silence* | Alexander Ryrie (2012) |
| FP173 | *On Tour in Byzantium: Excerpts from The Spiritual Meadow of John Moschus* | Ralph Martin SSM (2013) |
| FP174 | *Monastic Life* | Bonnie Thurston (2016) |
| FP175 | *Shall All Be Well? Reflections for Holy Week* | Graham Ward (2015) |
| FP176 | *Solitude and Communion: Papers on the Hermit Life* | ed. A. M. Allchin (2015) |
| FP177 | *The Prayers of Jacob of Serugh* | ed. Mary Hansbury (2015) |
| FP178 | *The Monastic Hours of Prayer* | Sr Benedicta Ward SLG (2016) |
| FP179 | *The Desert of the Heart: Daily Readings with the Desert Fathers* | trans. Sr Benedicta Ward SLG (2016) |
| FP180 | *In Company with Christ: Lent, Palm Sunday, Good Friday & Easter to Pentecost* | Sr Benedicta Ward SLG (2016) |
| FP181 | *Lazarus: Come Out! Reflections on John 11* | Bonnie Thurston (2017) |
| FP182 | *Unknowing & Astonishment: Meditations on Faith for the Long Haul* | Christopher Scott (2018) |
| FP183 | *Pondering, Praying, Preaching: Romans 8* | Bonnie Thurston (2/2021) |
| FP184 | *Shem`on the Graceful: Discourse on the Solitary Life* | trans. with introd. Mary Hansbury (2020) |
| FP185 | *God Under my Roof: Celtic Songs and Blessings* (revised and enlarged edition) | Esther de Waal (2020) |
| FP186 | *Journeying with the Jesus Prayer* | James. F. Wellington (2020) |
| FP187 | *Poet of the Word: Re-reading Scripture with Ephraem the Syrian* | Aelred Partridge OC (2020) |
| FP188 | *Identity and Ritual* | Alan Griffiths (2021) |
| FP189 | *River of the Spirit: The Spirituality of Simon Barrington-Ward* | Andy Lord (2021) |
| FP190 | *Prayer and the Struggle Against Evil* | John Barton, Daniel Lloyd, James Ramsay, Alexander Ryrie (2021) |
| FP191 | *Dante's Spiritual Journey: A Reading of the Divine Comedy* | Tony Dickinson (2021) |
| FP192 | *Jesus the Undistorted Image of God* | John Townroe (2021) |
| FP200 | *Monastic Vocation* | SISTERS OF THE LOVE OF GOD, Archbp Rowan Williams (2021) |

### Contemplative Poetry Series

CP1 *Amado Nervo: Poems of Faith and Doubt* trans. John Gallas (2021)
CP2 *Anglo-Saxon Poets: The High Roof of Heaven* trans. John Gallas (2021)
CP3 *Middle English Poets: Where Grace Grows Ever Green* trans. and ed. John Gallas (2021)

### Vestry Guides

VG1 *The Visiting Minister: How to Welcome Visiting Clergy to your Church* Paul Monk (2021)

**slgpress.co.uk**